When My Grandma Went to Heaven

Sebastian Leipold & Lukas Leipold

With Malissa Scheuring Leipold

Archway Publishing books may be ordered through booksellers or by contacting:

Archway Publishing
1663 Liberty Drive
Bloomington, IN 47403
www.archwaypublishing.com
844-669-3957

ISBN: 978-1-6657-2359-6 (sc)
ISBN: 978-1-6657-2358-9 (hc)
ISBN: 978-1-6657-2360-2 (e)

Print information available on the last page.

Archway Publishing rev. date: 05/18/2022

This book is dedicated to our Grandma who taught us that
life is not just about us, but about the love we share and
the smiles that we put on other people's faces.

When I was born, my Grandma was there. She always told me stories of how she hugged and kissed me just minutes after I came into this life. She never tired of whispering to me how much I was loved by her and God.

My Grandma stayed with me for the first week of my life. She sat on the couch in our living room and held me tight all day long. She talked to me about how special I am and how I was meant for great things in this life.

When I was just a few years old, my Grandma started to have trouble seeing the smile on my face and my big brown eyes. She would tell me that she could still see me in a blurry way, especially when I wore my bright red shirt. But my Grandma assured me that it was okay because she could close her eyes and see my face whenever she wanted.

Soon my Grandma couldn't see much at all except for shadows and light. This made it hard for her to walk since she was scared that she might trip on something and fall, so I would hold her arm as we would walk. At mealtimes I would sit at the kitchen table and help her find the food on her plate with her fork. She would tell me how much this helped her.

6

One day I was really worried when my Pa and Mom had to call the ambulance when we were at my Pa and Grandma's house. My Grandma was so weak she couldn't get up out of her comfortable chair or talk to me. This made me so scared. The ambulance workers tried to reassure me that they would take good care of my Grandma, but all I knew was that I couldn't do anything for her and I wasn't old enough to go with her to the hospital. I stood with my Mom and older brother Lukas out in front of the house as the ambulance pulled away and we just cried.

When I was 6 years old I knew my Grandma really needed us. I would snuggle right next to her in her chair and hold on tight under the soft, fuzzy blanket. I loved this the most.

Then before I knew it, my Grandma was back in the hospital again. I knew it wasn't good since my Mom didn't say too much. After a couple of days, we went to the hospital with my Mom and waited for another ambulance to come pick Grandma up to take her to a hospice. My Mom explained to me that this is a beautiful place where loving people will help us make Grandma comfortable and where we would love her until God brings her to heaven. It sounded like a nice, peaceful place to me, but I didn't really think about what it all meant.

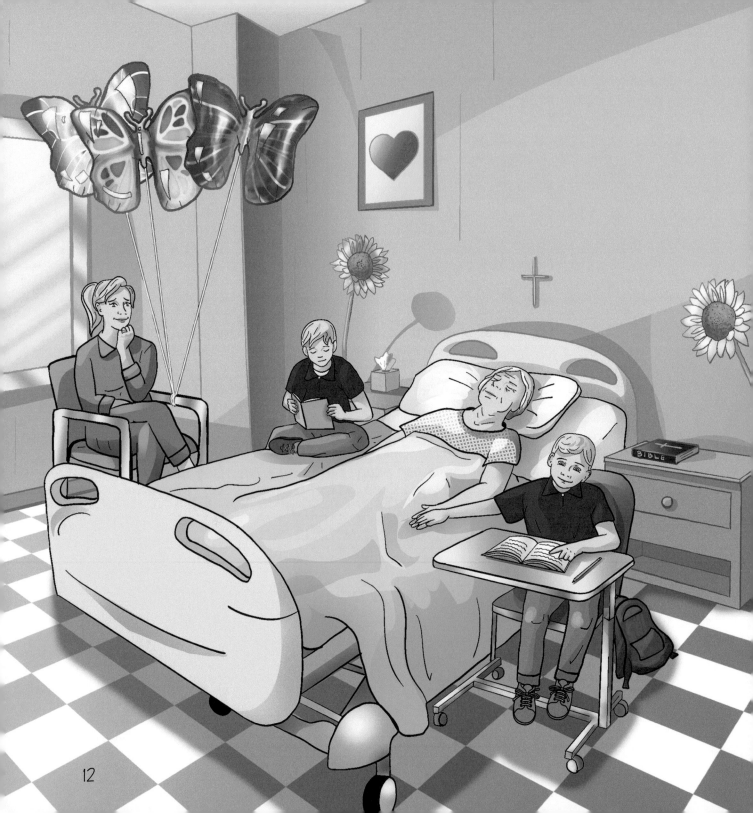

For two weeks my Mom would pick me and my brother Lukas up from school and we would go be with my Grandma in her room. We tried making it look cheerful and a little bit like home. We brought her big butterfly balloons and balloons of big smiley faces on which we wrote messages about our love for her and God's love for her too. We even brought her huge sunflowers which we placed on both sides of her bed which made the room look like one big flower garden. It was now our home too.

My Mom would help us with our homework on Grandma's bed, and we would take turns hugging her and whispering into her ears how much we loved her. Sometimes we would lie next to her and try to cuddle with her as she slept. My Mom would sing to her and tell her stories about growing up, all the while reminding her that she was the best Mom ever. It was sometimes hard for me to stay in the room and see my Mom's tears and how much she already missed Grandma.

One afternoon I saw a tiny fly in my Grandma's room and I got so worried for her since she would sometimes sleep with her mouth open. I remembered that my Mom had once bought me and my brother Lukas a plant which would eat tiny bugs like this. That night my Mom promised that we would try to find one for Grandma on the way home...and we did. It was a Venus Fly Trap plant.

The next day I placed the plant in Grandma's room and it made me feel so good. I felt like I had finally done something to protect her, and it filled me with joy. I was so happy that I decided it was time to take walks around the hospital floor and see what was happening. Since I love to talk to people, I found myself telling the family in the room across the hall about the Venus Fly Trap plant. Before I knew it I went back to my Grandma's room with enough money to buy five plants for other families on the same hospital floor. That night we again went back to the store and bought five more plants and delivered them to the patients' rooms the next day.

As the days passed, the word spread about my gift of the plants. My Mom did her best to help me with my new project of trying to help the families of other patients protect the people they loved. I found a purpose, and I saw the smiles through the tears on the people's faces whom I visited with plants. One mother of a young boy who was there told me that I was brighter than the sun because I brought so much light into the darkness of their lives. I began to wonder if this was part of the reason my Grandma was here and why she was holding on for so long when the doctors kept telling us that she should have already gone to heaven.

It was now a Thursday and it seemed like any other day that we had been living for the past 2 weeks. My Mom picked us up from school early so we could spend the afternoon with our Grandma. Mom was a little more anxious this time, which made me worry. When we got into the car, my brother said to my Mom that right before he was called out of his classroom, he heard Grandma's voice call his name, "Lukas." Mom told him that she always knew Grandma was especially close to him and she knew he would be listening, so it may have very well been her voice talking to his heart.

18

When we arrived at the hospital, Grandma's door was closed. This was different since the door was always wide open. We walked over to her door and opened it together. My Pa was there sitting next to Grandma's bed and I knew that my Grandma was no longer there. My Mom sat on her bed and held her close in her arms as she cried. I could tell through her tears that my Mom knew that Grandma was okay now since God would have been so very loving and gentle as he came to pick her up and bring her home to Him in heaven. It was time.

I sometimes get angry and ask my Mom why my Grandma had to leave us and go to heaven when I was so young. I would say that I hardly knew her. After all, I was only 6 years old when she went to heaven. But my Mom would tell me that God must have thought that this was just enough time for me to know how much I was loved by her.

Since that time, I have not forgotten my purpose there where my Grandma went to heaven. I still go back with my Mom and Lukas to visit dying patients and their families and bring them a Venus Fly Trap with hopes of a smile, and I have seen many.

Sometimes I wonder what my purpose is in this life. My Mom always says that God created me to do something that only I was created to do, and I have really come to believe that. Even though my Grandma was so sick, I believe she stuck around knowing that I had a job to do – to bring smiles to the dying.

I experienced so much love simply because of my Grandma. Like Mom said, maybe 6 years together was enough because I now know that it is okay to suffer with the people you love and it is great to be happy with those you love. My heart is also happy because I know I am doing what God created me to do in my special way.

Epilogue

. . . .

Since September 2018, Sebastian, along with the help of his Mom, Malissa, and his older brother, Lukas, have raised money to purchase over 200 Venus Fly Trap plants to continue his project to bring smiles to the dying. And as far as Sebastian is concerned, this is something he will do for many days to come. His Grandma is smiling from above for sure.

Printed in the United States
by Baker & Taylor Publisher Services